D1217513

Abuse and Neglect

By Sarah Medina

Health Consultant: John G. Samanich, M.D.

Gareth Stevens
Publishing

A WEEKLY READER COMPANY

Please visit our web site at **www.garethstevens.com.**
For a free color catalog describing Gareth Stevens
Publishing's list of high-quality books, call
1-800-542-2595 (USA) or 1-800-387-3178 (Canada).
Gareth Stevens Publishing's fax: 1-877-542-2596

Library of Congress Cataloging in Publication Data
Medina, Sarah, 1960-
  Abuse and neglect / Sarah Medina ; health consultant, John
G. Samanich. — North American ed.
     p. cm. — (Emotional health issues)
  Includes bibliographical references and index.
  ISBN-13: 978-0-8368-9198-0 (lib. bdg.)
  ISBN-10: 0-8368-9198-8 (lib. bdg.)
  1. Child abuse. 2. Child sexual abuse.
3. Psychological child abuse. 4. Abused children. I. Title.
HV6626.5.M43   2009
362.76—dc22   2008005458

This North American edition first published in 2009 by
Gareth Stevens Publishing
A Weekly Reader® Company
1 Reader's Digest Road
Pleasantville, NY 10570-7000 USA

This U.S. edition copyright © 2009 by Gareth Stevens, Inc.
Original edition copyright © 2008 by Wayland. First published in Great Britain in 2008
by Wayland, 338 Euston Road, London NW1 3BH, United Kingdom.

Series Editor: Nicola Edwards   Consultant: Peter Evans
Designer: Alix Wood   Picture Researcher: Kathy Lockley

Gareth Stevens Managing Editor: Lisa M. Herrington
Gareth Stevens Senior Editor: Barbara Bakowski
Gareth Stevens Creative Director: Lisa Donovan

Photo credits: G.M.B. Akash/Panos Pictures: 7b; John Angerson/Alamy: 16; Paul Baldesare/Photofusion:
title page, 10; Emely/zefa/Corbis: 44; Randy Faris/Corbis: 8; Maurizio Gamberini/dpa/Corbis: 7t;
Gianni Giansanti/Sygma/Corbis: 29; Kirsty-Anne Glubish/Design Pics/Corbis: 15; image100/Corbis:
11, 40; Image Source/Corbis: 17, 39; Le Studio/AgenceImage/Jupiterimages: 14; Lucidio Studio,
Inc./Corbis: 35; Roy McMahon/Corbis: 4; Nonstock/JupiterImages: 34; Ulrike Preuss/Photofusion:
Cover, 42; Ivy Reynolds/Botanica/Jupiterimages: 30; Benjamin Rondel/Corbis: 5; Sciencephotos/Alamy:
18; Ian Scrivener/Alamy: 28; Wishlist: 9, 12, 20, 21, 23, 24, 25, 27, 31, 32, 33, 36, 38, 41, 43, 45

Printed in China
1 2 3 4 5 6 7 8 9 10 09 08

The information in this
book is not intended to
substitute for professional
medical or psychological
care. The case studies are
based on real experiences,
but the names are fictitious.
All people in the photos are
models except where a
caption specifically names
an individual.

Contents

Words that appear in **boldface** type are in the glossary on page 46.

Introduction

Brenda's boyfriend says she does everything wrong. He calls her fat, ugly, and lazy, and he becomes angry when she wants to spend time with her family and friends. Brenda feels lonely, trapped, and miserable in this relationship.

Every day, 14-year-old Carlos's parents hit him. He often has cuts and bruises, but he always finds an excuse to cover up what happened. Carlos is terrified; recently, his father tried to strangle him. Carlos feels worthless and often thinks about how he can end his life.

Laura, 18, was abused by her uncle when she was 12. He made her touch private parts of his body, and he touched her body inappropriately. He told Laura the touching was "their secret" and threatened to hurt her if she told anyone. Laura has never had a boyfriend; she feels ashamed, and she is afraid that men are going to hurt her.

Omar lives alone and has a physical **disability**. He needs help with personal care. His son's wife agreed to help him, but on some days she does not come until lunchtime. Omar is left in bed, feeling hungry and uncomfortable. Omar has not told his son; he does not want to burden him. Every night, Omar goes to sleep hoping that he will not wake up in the morning.

Abuse can take many forms. Within a relationship, physical abuse may be combined with emotional abuse and can cause anxiety, fear, and unhappiness.

Elderly or ill people who are physically frail are particularly at risk for abusive treatment by others.

What is abuse?

Abuse is cruel and hurtful treatment of another person. There are four main types of abuse. **Emotional abuse**, as in Brenda's case, damages a person's feelings. **Physical abuse** causes harm to someone's body, like Carlos's. **Sexual abuse** is sexual contact that is forced on someone, like Laura. **Neglect**, as in Omar's case, is a form of abuse in which someone's physical or emotional needs are ignored.

Abuse can occur anywhere: at home, school, or work; in institutions, such as nursing homes or day care facilities; and out in the community. Abuse can be carried out by anyone, even by someone who should give love and care, such as a family member. Certain people—such as elderly or ill individuals, people with disabilities, and children—are especially **vulnerable** to abusers.

Find out more

This book focuses on the many long-lasting physical and **psychological** effects of abuse on young people. The first chapter deals with children's rights and needs. Other chapters describe the four main forms of abuse. Finally, there is advice on how to prevent abuse and how to find help and support for victims of abuse and neglect.

It's a fact:
child abuse

- Approximately 40 million children below the age of 15 suffer child abuse each year, according to the World Health Organization.

5

Chapter 1: *Children's rights and needs*

Governments make laws to ensure that people's rights are protected. There are special laws to protect children's rights. It is important for young people to know their rights. That knowledge helps them recognize what is—and what is not—acceptable behavior and treatment.

The U.N. Convention on the Rights of the Child

The United Nations (U.N.) Convention on the Rights of the Child is one of the most important international agreements for children. Adopted in 1989, it is a list of rights that all children should have. So far, more than 190 countries, all over the globe, have signed the agreement. Those countries have agreed to follow the guidelines in the agreement when making laws to protect children.

In focus: whose rights?

The U.N. Convention on the Rights of the Child says that everyone under the age of 18 has all the rights listed in the agreement. It applies to everyone, regardless of race, religion, language, abilities, financial situation, or family background.

What does the U.N. Convention say?

The U.N. Convention on the Rights of the Child covers many areas of life that involve children, including school, work, and play. It starts by setting out the most basic right: the right to life. The document then goes on to list many other basic rights that all children should have.

Some parts of the U.N. Convention deal directly with the issues of child abuse and neglect. For example, the convention says that governments should protect children from violence, abuse, and neglect by their parents or by anyone else who looks after them. Governments should also guard children from sexual abuse and from dangerous drugs.

It's a fact:
the U.N. Convention on the Rights of the Child

The list of rights includes these:

- Children have the right to good-quality health care, clean water, nutritious food, and a clean environment so that they can stay healthy.

- Children have the right to an education.

- Children have the right to relax and play and to join in a variety of different activities.

- Parents should always consider what is best for each child.

- Governments should protect children from work that might hurt them in any way.

People under 18 years old often need special care and protection that adults do not. The healthy development of children is important to the future of our society. That is why the U.N. Convention is helping millions of young people by making sure that governments protect the rights of the young. As a result, local and national governments have made or changed laws so that they are in the best interests of children.

Some children are forced to work long hours in terrible conditions. This is a form of child abuse.

Children's needs

All children have basic needs, both physical and emotional. Parents and caregivers are responsible for looking after children's needs. When their needs are ignored, children suffer.

Physical needs

A child's most basic physical needs are food and drink. Children who have nothing to eat will die within weeks. Without a drink, they will die within days. Children also need a safe place to live and adequate clothes to wear. Good health care helps keep children well, and supervision keeps them safe from harm.

Emotional needs

Children need love and care just as they need food and drink. A warm, secure home life helps children develop **self-esteem**. Children who feel unloved or insecure feel bad about themselves. They may be unhappy, have trouble in school, and share difficult relationships with others.

Children need time and attention from their parents or caregivers so they know that they are loved. Respect helps children feel sure about

CASE STUDY

Jonathan hated gym classes at school. He was embarrassed because he often had bruises on his arms and legs. He worried that everyone would notice the marks and would laugh at him. He often tried to find reasons to be excused from gym.

One day, Jonathan's phys ed teacher took him aside and gently asked how he had gotten the bruises on his body. Jonathan burst into tears. He said that since his parents' divorce, his mother had been hitting him. He told the teacher that the violence was worse when his mom was tired or stressed. She just couldn't seem to control her temper.

Spending time together as a family makes children feel loved and valued.

Some people become aggressive after drinking alcohol. Drinking too much, however, is never an excuse for abusive behavior toward others.

themselves. Praise and encouragement make them want to succeed and to behave well. Guidance and appropriate discipline teach children right from wrong. Reassurance helps them feel safe when things go wrong.

Why does abuse happen?

There are many reasons why people abuse others. Some people who were abused when they were young may abuse their own children. They may think that abuse is "normal" behavior. Other people simply are unable to control themselves when they get angry, and they lash out at the people around them.

Stress or **depression** can cause some people to abuse others. If people are unhappy, they may not think about how they are making others unhappy. Some people behave abusively when they are experiencing the effects of alcohol or drug use.

Recognizing abuse

Sometimes, people do not realize that they are being abused. Knowing their rights and needs helps people recognize abuse. It is important to remember that help is available for victims. See page 38 for information about how to put a stop to abuse.

In focus: any excuse?

Although there may be a reason for someone's abusive behavior, there is never an excuse. Abusers are completely responsible for what they do. Abuse is never the victim's fault—and abuse is always wrong.

Chapter 2: *Emotional abuse*

Emotional abuse occurs when someone attacks the feelings of another person. This type of behavior is also known as psychological abuse, mental abuse, or verbal abuse. Emotional abuse is often carried out through words. It affects the way people think about themselves. Emotional abuse may not leave any outward physical signs, but it can leave deep and long-lasting scars within its victims.

What is emotional abuse?

Emotional abuse is at the core of all forms of abuse. Some people with disabilities or people from **ethnic minorities** are abused emotionally when others insult them or treat them inconsiderately. Adults who are unhappy in a relationship may emotionally abuse their partners by yelling at or insulting them. **Domestic violence** is an extreme form of emotional abuse (see page 14).

Children are vulnerable to emotional abuse, particularly when they witness violence between adults in the home. Children need love, care, and respect to feel safe and confident as they grow up. When their parents or caregivers are hurtful, young people often feel worthless and confused.

Young people who are emotionally abused may feel lost and lonely.

Children who experience emotional abuse at home may also be abused in

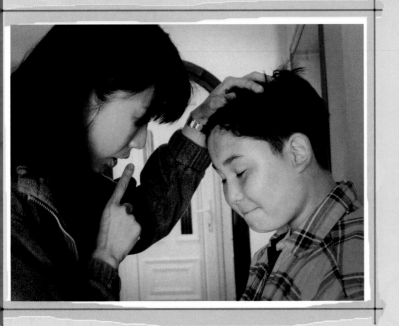

Some parents go too far when disciplining their children. That is where discipline becomes abuse.

other ways, too. Some parents emotionally abuse their children by telling them they are useless and unloved. At the same time, the parents may physically abuse the youngsters by hitting them. They may also lock the children in their rooms, ignore their needs, and refuse to give them anything to eat or drink.

While these parents may think that they are simply being strict and teaching their children a lesson, their actions are abusive and wrong. The most damaging effects of child abuse and neglect often result from the emotional, rather than the physical, aspects.

In focus: *how far is too far?*

Most people have arguments at some time. Family members may become annoyed with one another. At school, classmates sometimes argue. Anger is a normal feeling—but it is important that a person's anger does not hurt others. If someone's anger makes another person feel afraid or worthless, this is a case of emotional abuse.

CASE STUDY

Dina's older sister, Tanya, is lively, has a lot of friends, and gets good grades at school. Their parents buy Tanya nice clothes and spend time with her, taking her out to restaurants and movies. They pay little attention to Dina, though. They often leave her at home when they take Tanya out, telling Dina to do her homework or to clean her room. Although she tries hard to be good and to make her parents proud, she feels that they don't really love her. Dina has no self-confidence, and she is struggling at school. She feels lonely and sad.

How is emotional abuse carried out?

Emotional abuse takes many forms. It can occur when a parent purposely ignores a child and withholds affection. Emotional abuse can also result when a parent demands or expects too much from a child. Although these behaviors may seem contradictory, both are acts of emotional abuse.

Humiliating people by laughing at them is a form of emotional abuse. It can make victims feel isolated and vulnerable.

Shouting and frightening

Shouting is a common form of emotional abuse. While anger is a normal emotion, explosive expressions of anger can **intimidate** people, especially children. Many abusers want to frighten their victims. They may threaten to hurt young people or to abandon them. They may even damage their victims' belongings or attack their pets.

Criticism and humiliation

Abusers often make themselves feel better by making others feel bad. Abusers may use constant criticism or insults, saying that their victims do everything wrong or that no one cares about them. Abusers may blame their victims whenever things go wrong. They may humiliate people by calling them names or by teasing them cruelly. Abusers often say that they are "only joking"—but emotional abuse is not a joke.

It's a fact: bullying

- Most people think of bullying as physical abuse, such as pushing or hitting. Bullying can be a form of emotional abuse, too.

- Three out of four kids say they have been bullied or teased.

Withdrawal of love and attention

Emotional abuse can sometimes be more about what the abuser does *not* do than what he or she does. Some abusers refuse to show love to their victims. They may be cold toward a child or another family member who needs care and affection. Abusers may refuse to spend time with their victims. These behaviors leave children feeling rejected. Often, that outcome is exactly what the abuser seeks.

Isolation

Locking a child in a room is a way to isolate him or her—and it is another form of emotional abuse. An abuser can feel powerful by taking away a victim's right to be with other people. **Isolation** can also happen when the abuser stops the victim from seeing friends or taking part in activities outside school. The abuser seeks control over his or her victim.

Unreasonable demands

Sometimes people expect too much of others. An abusive parent may demand that a daughter get straight As on all her exams. A parent may expect a child to study all the time, even when he is tired, or may demand that he do a lot of heavy chores every day. Victims of demanding behavior often feel that they have to do everything perfectly.

Corruption of children

Adults sometimes emotionally abuse young people by **corrupting** them— that is, by encouraging unacceptable or harmful behavior. Some parents may allow their young children to use drugs or alcohol, even though such use is illegal and puts children's health at risk. Adults may ask children to commit crimes, such as stealing, or they may encourage fighting with other children.

Exploitation

Exploitation occurs when someone unfairly uses or forces someone else to do something for them. In some

CASE STUDY

Aatmaja, who is 11 years old, works in a factory in India. She starts at 4 A.M. and works 12 hours each day. Her work is exhausting, and the factory is dirty and noisy. Aatmaja does not have a bedroom—or even a bed. She sleeps on the grimy factory floor, between the heavy machines. She has only rice to eat and must pay her boss for that meager food.

Aatmaja sees her family only once a week, and she misses her parents and her siblings. She often dreams of being able to live at home and go to school.

Some people mistakenly believe that domestic violence affects only adults. However, children who see their parents or caregivers lashing out at each other can be frightened and troubled.

countries, children are forced to work from a very young age, often to pay family debts. They may be separated from their families while they work as servants or in factories. Some children are even forced to fight in wars.

In focus: *working children*

In developing countries, about 218 million children between the ages of five and 17 work, according to the organization Human Rights Watch. In some cases, a child's work can be a positive experience. However, children who work long hours, often in dangerous and unhealthy conditions, are at risk for lasting physical and psychological harm.

Domestic violence and children

In some families, domestic violence between parents or caregivers is a daily reality for children. Children may routinely hear or witness emotional or physical abuse by adults they love. Young people may even step in to try to stop the abuse. This is a particularly distressing and harmful form of emotional abuse for children.

Emotional abusers

People we live, study, or work with can do the most damage. Emotional abusers are usually people we expect to love or care for us. Most people who emotionally abuse others are older, bigger, or stronger than their victims. They are often in a position of power, such as a parent over a child or a teacher over a pupil.

Why do abusers do it?

Some parents find it difficult to accept their children as they are. Other parents have trouble dealing with the normal ups and downs of family life. They may be stressed by divorce or unemployment, for example, and they find it hard to control their feelings. They may have experienced abuse in their own childhood and have not yet recovered from that **trauma**. Older children may abuse their younger siblings because of jealousy. Some abusers have mental health problems, such as depression. They find it hard to respect the rights and needs of others. Other people who commit abuse are affected by alcohol or drugs.

Sometimes, people emotionally abuse others on purpose, because they want to control what their victim feels or does. Some emotional abuse is not deliberate—for example, when a parent yells at a child in a moment of stress. Often, people who emotionally abuse others blame their victims or make excuses for the behavior. It is important to remember that there is never an excuse for emotional abuse.

Emotional abuse can come from people teens care about, such as boyfriends or girlfriends.

What are the effects of emotional abuse?

Long-term emotional abuse is deeply damaging. It makes people feel unloved and unimportant. Even one insult can hurt a person for many years. The effects of abuse may not always show, but they are serious.

Sadness and depression

Victims of emotional abuse usually feel sad. They may hate themselves and become depressed. Life can seem hopeless. Depression may cause them to fall behind at school and withdraw from friends and fun activities.

Constant anxiety

Emotional abuse is very stressful. Because abusers are more powerful than their victims, victims often feel fear and loss of control. Some victims run away from home—sometimes more than once—because they cannot cope any longer.

Anger and aggression

Victims often feel angry, which can make them act aggressively. Antisocial behavior, such as lying or stealing, may become a problem.

Self-harm

Victims may feel so unhappy that they **self-harm**—for example, by abusing alcohol or drugs. Some people may engage in high-risk activities, such as driving too fast, which can indicate that

Some people are so desperate to feel relief from the agony of emotional abuse that they cut their arms so that they bleed.

Emotional abuse can make it hard for people to sleep, as the worry and fear go round and round in their minds.

It's a fact:
suicide

- Each year, about 32,000 Americans die by suicide. Almost 5,000 of them are under the age of 24.

- Each day, 14 people between the ages of 15 and 24 die by suicide. That is one young person every 100 minutes.

- Almost four times as many men as women die by suicide, according to the National Institute of Mental Health.

- Women and girls are three times as likely as men and boys to attempt suicide.

their self-esteem is low and that they do not respect themselves. Some victims cut themselves or harm their bodies in other ways. Some feel hopeless and decide to commit suicide.

Getting help

No one should have to suffer emotional abuse. It is important to know that help is available for victims. (See Chapter 6.)

Chapter 3: *Physical abuse*

Physical abuse occurs when someone hurts another person's body in some way, either causing, or having the potential to cause, injury. Injury can be caused by a range of actions, from pushing or hitting to poisoning a person. Some injuries are serious. In fact, physical abuse can—and sometimes does—lead to death. All injuries, including cuts and bruises that heal within a few days, are serious. No one deserves to be hurt in this way.

What is physical abuse?

Physical abuse is always a shock to the body and the mind of the victim. People who physically abuse others may commit other forms of abuse, too. For example, children who are emotionally abused (see page 10) may also be physically hurt. An older brother may kick a younger sibling while calling her stupid and useless.

A black eye can be a visible sign of physical abuse and the deep emotional pain it causes.

In focus: is spanking OK?

For many years, people have argued over the right of parents to spank their children. Is spanking an act of physical abuse, or is it an acceptable way for parents to discipline their children?

Nineteen countries have banned **corporal punishment**. Sweden was the first country to make spanking illegal. In England and Wales, parents who spank children so hard that it leaves a mark can be sent to prison for up to five years. In the United States, each state makes its own laws on corporal punishment. Many states allow parents to use "reasonable" physical force to discipline their children. Spanking by parents is not banned in any of the states.

People who support spanking say that it is a useful way for parents to discipline their children and that parents have the right to choose. Opponents argue that spanking is a form of physical abuse. They believe that it should be just as wrong to hit a child as it is to hit an adult.

A school bully may shove a victim while laughing and calling the person names. Adults may use physical abuse to frighten and control children they are sexually abusing (see page 26).

Often, physical abuse is something that happens regularly over a period of time. Some young people suffer physical abuse throughout their childhood. Sometimes, physical abuse happens during a stressful period— perhaps for a few weeks or a few months. Still, even a single incident of physical abuse—having one's hair pulled by a bully or being kicked by a parent or a caregiver, for example—can have long-lasting effects.

CASE STUDY

Donna's father was drunk when he grabbed her and pushed her against the kitchen wall. He yelled into Donna's face that she was lazy and stupid because she did not have dinner waiting for him when he got home. Donna was terrified. Her hand was twisted hard behind her back. For days afterward, her wrist was so bruised and swollen that she could hardly pick up her pen to do her schoolwork. Yet Donna did not tell anyone about her father's actions. She was too ashamed, and she did not want to get her father in trouble. She just tried to stay out of his way.

What does physical abuse involve?

People physically abuse others in many ways. Some actions, such as **suffocating** someone, are extreme and life-threatening. Other actions, such as pushing or shoving, may seem less serious but can be equally dangerous. A shove that results in a fall and a blow to the head can cause serious injury or even death.

Pushing or shaking

Pushing and shaking may not seem serious, but both actions are forms of physical abuse. People who are pushed may fall and be badly hurt. Shaking a baby or a small child can cause brain damage. That type of injury is known as **shaken baby syndrome**. Permanent disability or even death can occur.

Pinching, biting, or hair pulling

Some abusers pinch their victims, causing bruising or bleeding. Some people bite, puncturing the skin and sometimes causing an infection. Other abusers pull their victims' hair, sometimes hard enough to pull it out.

Hitting and beating

Hitting is a common form of physical abuse. Some abusers slap their victims with an open hand; others punch with their fists. Some abusers use an object, such as a wooden spoon or a belt, to beat their victims. Hitting and beating can cause injuries such as cuts, bruises, and swelling. A black eye can result from a blow to the head.

Physical abuse may occur regularly over a period of time. Some young people experience physical abuse throughout their childhood.

Kicking and throwing

A single kick to the foot or the leg can be very painful. When an abuser continues kicking, especially at the victim's head or face, serious harm can result, including the loss of an eye. Some abusers grab their victims and throw them against a door or a wall or onto the floor before kicking them.

Cutting and stabbing

Using knives to cut people is a dangerous form of physical abuse. Stabbing can be life-threatening, especially when an internal organ, such as the heart or the liver, is pierced. Stab wounds can cause people to bleed to death.

Threatening and pushing or shoving someone is behavior that combines bullying with physical abuse. People with disabilities can be targets for abusers.

It's a fact:
physical punishment

- According to the World Health Organization, more than 80 percent of children in many countries across the world experience physical punishment in their homes.

- In 2006, the United Nations Global Study on Violence as well as the United Nations Committee on the Rights of the Child called for the prohibition of corporal punishment.

Poisoning

Another form of physical abuse is intentional poisoning. Most cases of poisoning happen to children younger than three. They may be poisoned with alcohol, prescription drugs, or over-the-counter medications. Some abusers poison people with household items or other common chemicals, such as bleach, detergents, floor cleaners, weed killers, and antifreeze. Some victims are poisoned with salt. Too much salt can cause serious illness, brain damage, and death.

Even water can be used as a form of poison. A small number of abusers force their victim, usually a young child, to drink large quantities of water. The child may experience confusion, **nausea**, and vomiting. Eventually, too much water in the body causes sodium (salt) levels to drop, resulting in swelling of the brain. **Seizures**, **coma**, and even death can occur.

Burning or scalding

Victims of physical abuse may be scarred permanently by burns from a cigarette, an iron, a hot stove, or a flame. Some abusers scald young victims by placing them in a bath of extremely hot water. Many victims of burning or scalding need treatment at a hospital. Very severe burns can sometimes lead to death.

Choking, drowning, or suffocating

When victims are choked, drowned, or suffocated, they are unable to breathe. Choking happens when an abuser puts his or her hands around a victim's neck to strangle the person. Drowning occurs when a victim's head is held underwater. Suffocation is an uncommon but serious form of child abuse. Some abusers smother their victims by covering their noses and mouths with a pillow, a blanket, or a plastic bag. Choking, drowning, and suffocating are particularly deadly forms of abuse.

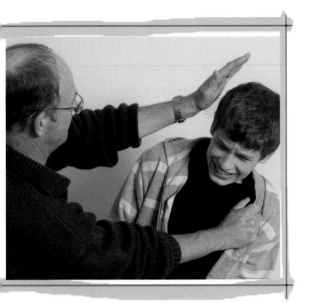

Striking someone on the head can cause serious injury.

Bullying

Bullying happens in many settings—at home, at school, and at work. Some adults bully other adults, but bullying usually occurs between children. Bullies may use emotional abuse to make their victims feel bad about themselves. Bullies may also physically abuse others, pushing, hitting, or kicking them to cause pain and fright. Bullying can be a terrifying experience. It is abuse, and it is unacceptable.

Who carries out physical abuse?

Physical abusers are usually people who are close to the victim. They include parents, siblings, boyfriends, and girlfriends. Some caregivers physically abuse vulnerable people they look after, such as young children, elderly or ill individuals, or people with disabilities.

Why do people abuse others?

Parents and caregivers may not believe that their actions are physical abuse. They may think that hitting their children is an acceptable form of discipline. Stress or depression can also lead to physical abuse. Some people struggle to cope as they care for children or elderly relatives. People with personal problems, such as divorce or unemployment, sometimes physically abuse others to feel in control. Alcohol or other drugs may also be a factor. Finally, people who were abused as children are more likely to become abusers themselves.

CASE STUDY

When 12-year old Miranda's friends started to smoke cigarettes, Miranda went along with them, just to be part of the group. One day, her mother found cigarettes in Miranda's bureau drawer. She was furious. She yelled at Miranda and slapped her hard across her face. Since then, she has hit Miranda repeatedly, often leaving bruises. Miranda is hurt and frightened by her mother's behavior. She thinks that her mom no longer loves her.

What are the effects of physical abuse?

Physical abuse can lead to serious injury. Thousands of children die every year from injuries caused by abuse. Physical abuse affects more than the body, however. Victims suffer deep emotional scars, which heal much more slowly than physical damage.

Physical injury

Injuries caused by physical abuse can vary. Shoving, hitting, and kicking can result in cuts, bruises, black eyes, and broken bones and teeth. Some abusers pull their victim's hair so hard that it comes out. Stabbing can damage internal organs, such as kidneys, and cause a great deal of blood loss. Shaking and poisoning can bring about brain damage, and burns often leave permanent scars. Many forms of physical abuse can lead to death.

Stress, anxiety, and fear

Many victims of physical abuse experience a great deal of stress. They worry constantly about the next episode of abuse. Even though abuse is never the victim's fault, he or she may act very cautiously, afraid to set off another attack. Many people who are abused have nightmares or sleep problems. Their schoolwork and their performance in sports and other activities may suffer because they are so tired.

Social problems

Victims of physical abuse often find it hard to trust people or form friendships. Some victims fear physical contact, startle easily, and become withdrawn. Others feel angry and take out their rage

When people are coping with physical mistreatment, they may feel isolated and unable to tell others about the abuse.

People who are being physically abused may turn to alcohol or drugs in an attempt to ease the emotional pain they feel.

on themselves or people around them. They may try to ease their emotional pain by engaging in self-harm—cutting, burning, or hurting their bodies in other ways. They may become bullies or begin to lie, steal, or abuse drugs and alcohol.

Low self-esteem

Physical abuse makes victims feel ashamed. They may believe that they are worthless and that no one will ever love them. Low self-esteem can develop into severe depression. Some victims of physical abuse commit suicide.

Getting help

No one should have to suffer physical abuse. It is important to remember that help is available for victims of physical abuse. (See Chapter 6.)

It's a fact:
physical abuse

- In 2005, at least 899,000 children in the United States were victims of abuse or neglect. Almost 17 percent of them experienced physical abuse.

- Each day, about four U.S. children die from abuse or neglect.

Chapter 4: *Sexual abuse*

Sexual abuse occurs when someone is forced by another person into sexual acts or situations. Sexual abuse can happen to children or adults. Any sexual contact between an older person and a child is sexual abuse. Sexual abuse can also occur between people of similar ages. Sexual abusers often use physical or emotional abuse to control their victims.

What is sexual abuse?

There are three main types of sexual abuse: non-touching sexual abuse, sexual touching, and sexual exploitation. In non-touching sexual abuse, a person may force a victim to look at sexual parts of the abuser's body or to watch sexual acts. Some sexual abusers force their victims to look at sexual images or videos, called **pornography**. They may talk to their victims about sexual things in a way that is frightening or embarrassing.

A person who is kissed or touched in a sexual way against his or her wishes is also being sexually abused. Sometimes the victim is made to kiss or touch the abuser sexually, too. Rape occurs when sexual intercourse is forced on someone. Rape can occur within a dating relationship and even within a marriage.

Sexual exploitation happens when an abuser forcibly takes sexually **explicit**

It's a fact: sexual abuse

- Every year, more than a million children worldwide are sexually exploited. They are forced to become **prostitutes**, sold for sexual purposes, or used in child pornography, according to the United Nations.

- The National Child Abuse and Neglect Data System found that more than 83,000 children were sexually abused in the United States in 2005. That number equals about 9 percent of child abuse and neglect cases in that year.

- Girls are more often the victims of sexual abuse.

photographs of a child. Some abusers make sexual videos involving children. Others force children to have sexual contact with people in exchange for money.

It can be difficult for people to talk about sexual abuse. However, the sexual abuse of children happens every day. Sexual abuse does not discriminate. It affects all social classes, races, and religions. All forms of sexual abuse are serious—and illegal.

Sexual abuse is extremely damaging to victims and can be especially terrifying for children. The effects of sexual abuse extend far beyond childhood. Many victims take years to recover from sexual abuse.

CASE STUDY

Fifteen-year-old Rachel had been going out with Dan, 19, for four months. Rachel thought that she was in love with Dan. He seemed nice, and they had a lot of fun together. Rachel enjoyed kissing Dan, but she did not want to take their physical relationship further. Dan said he understood and respected her wishes.

One night, he drove Rachel to a secluded place, where he raped her. Rachel was devastated. She started to miss classes and fell behind in her schoolwork. She did not want to go out with her friends, and she avoided spending time with her family. Rachel felt deeply ashamed. She thought it was her fault that Dan had raped her.

Although strangers sometimes carry out sexual abuse, most victims know their abusers. Being with a relative who wants to carry out sexual abuse is very frightening.

In focus: sex and the law

Many countries have laws to protect young people from sexual abuse and exploitation. In the United States, sexual activity of any kind between an adult and a person under a specific minimum age (which varies according to state law) is illegal.

Non-touching sexual abuse

Non-touching sexual abuse involves looking at the private parts of someone's body without his or her agreement. **Indecent exposure** occurs when an abuser exposes himself or herself to a victim. Some sexual abusers spy on children who are dressing or bathing. Others force their victims to undress in front of them.

Talking about sexual things is also a form of non-touching sexual abuse.

Abusers may make sexual comments to young people, causing them to have uncomfortable feelings. Sexual abusers sometimes force children or teens to listen to stories that involve sex. Some abusers use e-mail or text messages to send sexual messages to their victims.

Pornography is sexually explicit material, including pictures and words. Sexual abusers may force their victims to look at pornographic magazines, photographs, movies, or

Sexual abusers sometimes send explicit text messages and images to their victims.

Internet sites. Sometimes, victims are forced to watch or listen to other people in sexual situations.

Sexual touching

Touching forms of sexual abuse include kissing. Kissing may be on the mouth or on other parts of the body. Sexual abusers may touch private parts of the victim's body.

Sometimes, victims are made to touch private parts of the abuser's body. Young people may be forced to touch their own bodies while the abusers watch. Victims may also be raped, or forced to have sexual intercourse. Rape can cause serious injuries to victims.

Sexual exploitation

In the United States, most victims of sexual exploitation are runaways or abandoned children who live on the streets. Some sexual abusers force people, including children, to become prostitutes. Victims are made to have sexual contact with people in exchange for money.

Other abusers force their victims into pornography. Child pornography includes photographs or films of children while they are not wearing clothes or while they are doing something sexual. Abusers may view child pornography themselves or give or sell it to others.

Each year, thousands of young people are forced to become prostitutes. Some are kidnapped and taken far from their homes.

In focus: exploited for sex

It is estimated that about 293,000 American children and teenagers are currently at risk of becoming victims of sexual exploitation. Many young people who live on the streets are forced into prostitution. Their abusers often provide them with fake identification to use in the event of an arrest.

Dating is part of growing up, and curiosity about a partner's body is normal. Forcing a partner to engage in sexual activity against his or her will, however, is sexual abuse—and it is wrong. Sexual abuse makes victims feel uncomfortable, confused, or afraid. A healthy relationship is based on caring, not control.

Dating and sexual abuse

Sexual abuse sometimes happens when people are dating. Some people mistake abuse for love. They may even find the attention flattering. However, sexual abuse is not about love; it is about control. Love involves care and respect for another person.

Warning signs of sexual abuse within a relationship include any kind of unwanted sexual advances. Boyfriends and girlfriends sometimes have different ideas about the relationship. Expressions like "If you loved me, you would ..." are used to pressure or intimidate people. Teens should always follow their instincts about a situation. If it does not feel right, it isn't.

CASE STUDY

John, age 13, is scared to be around his uncle. Whenever Uncle Stan comes to visit, he tries to find ways to be alone with John. When they are alone, Uncle Stan talks about sex, which makes John feel really uncomfortable.

At times, he has noticed his uncle watching him, which makes John feel confused. On a couple of occasions, Uncle Stan has "accidentally" walked into John's bedroom while John was undressing. John has not told his parents because he is worried that they will not believe him. He thinks that his parents will believe Uncle Stan because he is an adult.

Who carries out sexual abuse?

A common image of a sexual abuser is a creepy adult in a raincoat hanging around in a park. Most sexual abusers, however, do not fit this image. They may be respected members of the community, such as religious leaders, coaches, or teachers. They may be childcare professionals. Many sexual abusers are men, but women can be sexually abusive, too.

Although strangers sometimes carry out sexual abuse, most victims know and trust their abusers. An abuser may be a friend, a neighbor, or a family member, such as a parent, sibling, grandparent, or cousin. Sexual abuse may happen just once, or it may continue for a long time. It usually happens in private.

Why do some people sexually abuse others?

Some people who were sexually abused when they were young grow up to abuse others. They may not know how to have a loving relationship. Some abusers find children sexually attractive. They may target children to feel more powerful. Sexual abusers may feel stressed or inadequate. They may abuse alcohol or other drugs.

Sexual abuse is often about power and control. It is never about love. Although there may be reasons that people sexually abuse others, there is never an excuse.

An adult's inappropriate attention to a younger person may be a warning sign of sexual abuse.

What are the effects of sexual abuse?

Even a single incident of sexual abuse can have serious and long-lasting effects on victims. Sexual abuse deeply damages victims' self-esteem, and it often hurts their relationships with other people.

Shame and confusion

People often feel ashamed after experiencing sexual abuse. They may feel "dirty" and wash themselves frequently in an effort to "wash away" the abuse. Sexual abuse can be very confusing, too. Abusers may say that they love their victims and that the abusive behavior is normal. Some abusers accuse their victims of "asking for" the abuse, perhaps blaming the victim for wearing revealing clothing. It is important to remember that sexual abuse is never about love and that victims always deserve help.

Fear and depression

Victims often feel afraid of their abusers and may feel afraid of other people, too. They may be scared to let anyone touch them—even a doctor. People who are sexually abused may feel sad, angry, and alone. Those feelings can lead to depression.

Social problems

Sometimes, victims react to sexual abuse with **antisocial behavior**, such as shoplifting or starting fires. They may be disruptive at school. Relationships may become difficult, because victims no longer trust other people. People who are sexually abused sometimes stop participating in activities they once enjoyed.

Preoccupation with sex

Children who are victims of sexual abuse sometimes behave in a sexual

Young people who have been sexually abused may wash obsessively in an attempt to cleanse themselves of their feelings of shame.

way with other people. For example, they may kiss people on the mouth in situations where that behavior is inappropriate. As adults, they may have many sexual partners and destructive or unstable relationships.

Physical impacts

Sexual abuse can cause physical injury, such as cuts and bruises. Rape can lead to unwanted pregnancy for girls and women. It can also lead to **sexually transmitted diseases** (STDs) or **human immunodeficiency virus** (HIV) infection. HIV is the virus that causes **acquired immune deficiency syndrome** (AIDS).

Self-harm

Victims of sexual abuse sometimes hate their own bodies. They may stop taking care of themselves. They may start to abuse alcohol or other drugs. Some victims cut or burn themselves. Others commit suicide.

Some teens who are sexually abused run away from home. They think running away is their only escape. Running away puts young people in danger, however. It is never the solution.

It's a fact: rape

- Rape can result in pregnancy. Girls under the age of 15 are five times as likely to die during pregnancy and childbirth as women in their twenties.

Getting help

No one should have to experience sexual abuse. It is important to remember that help is available. (See Chapter 6.)

Chapter 5: *Neglect*

Neglect is a form of abuse. It occurs when people fail to look after the basic needs of a person for whom they are responsible. Sometimes, parents neglect their children. Caregivers may neglect elderly or ill individuals or people with physical, mental, or emotional disabilities.

What is neglect?

If children are to grow into healthy adults, their parents or other caregivers must take responsibility for their physical and emotional needs. The consequences of child neglect are serious and can last a lifetime.

Physical needs

A child's most basic physical need is for a balanced and nutritious diet. Children also need a warm, dry, clean, and safe place to live and sleep. Clean clothes that are suitable for the weather are basic necessities, too.

Good **hygiene** helps children stay healthy, as does access to good medical and dental care. Children also need fresh air and exercise, balanced with plenty of rest.

Proper supervision helps children stay safe. When young people are out of the home, parents should always know

Home should be a safe haven for children, and the place where their emotional and physical needs are met.

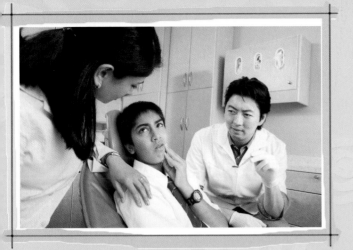

Providing regular dental care is one of the many ways in which parents and other caregivers should look after children's physical needs.

their children's whereabouts and their companions. Adults should also know when kids and teens will return home. Parents should impose reasonable rules of behavior for their children.

Emotional needs

A caring home life is necessary for children to develop into responsible adults with healthy self-esteem. When parents show affection and spend time with their children, the children know that they are loved. If parents or caregivers claim to love their children but do not show it, the children experience emotional neglect.

In focus: wants versus needs

Should children be given everything they want, such as the newest computers, cell phones, and electronic gadgets? Some parents think so. However, good parenting is not about satisfying children's wants but about fulfilling their needs.

Adults who respect young people—by listening to what they say and speaking to them respectfully—help children develop positive self-worth. Giving encouragement and praise helps young people feel valued and inspires them to succeed.

Education is essential for people to play a full part in the world. Parents have an important role in teaching children right from wrong and giving appropriate discipline, if necessary.

CASE STUDY

After Leah's parents separated, her mother started going out on dates. She sometimes left 11-year-old Leah at home to look after her younger brother, Adam. One time, the children were left at home all weekend while their mother went on a trip. She gave Leah a few dollars and told her to "be good" and to take care of Adam. A neighbor noticed that the children seemed to be on their own and called the police. Leah's mother had to be taught that leaving the children alone was dangerous.

Effects of neglect

Neglect can harm children's physical and emotional development. Without proper physical care, they may become ill. Without emotional care, they feel unloved and insecure. Over time, they feel unworthy of love and attention. Those feelings can harm their sense of self-worth and can damage future relationships. Many experts believe that the effects of neglect may last longer than the effects of other forms of abuse

Physical effects

Children who are neglected may fail to visit the doctor for checkups or get medical attention for injuries. They sometimes lack medicines that they need to take. Some victims of neglect get frequent colds o infections. They may have poor hygiene, too: Some children are dirty or have bad breath and body odor. Their

Some neglected children must pick through other people's trash to find food when they are hungry. Other youngsters may steal from stores or beg for food from people who pass by.

clothes may be dirty, old, or torn. Neglected children can feel tired all the time, making it hard for them to concentrate or do well at school.

Some neglected children are often hungry, and they may steal food or money from other people. They sometimes search through garbage pails to find scraps to eat. Some of these young people suffer from **malnutrition**.

Neglect in early stages of life can result in severe, long-term, and irreversible damage. Each year, more children die from neglect than from any other form of abuse.

Emotional effects

Neglected children often have low self-esteem. Because they feel unloved, they do not know how to value or care for themselves. They often withdraw from

other people and from activities that most kids think are fun. Children who are neglected may become depressed. Sometimes they become overly dependent on other people. Lack of confidence can make it hard for them to make their own way in the world.

Children who suffer from neglect may experience a variety of emotional and behavioral difficulties. They are at risk for committing crimes and abusing drugs and alcohol.

Getting help

No one should have to suffer neglect. It is important to know that help is available. (See Chapter 6.)

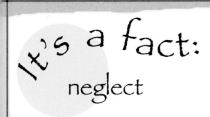

It's a fact:
neglect

- In 2005, more than 40 percent of child abuse deaths in the United States were caused by neglect.

- Risk for neglect is highest among children younger than five years old.

Chapter 6: *Getting help*

All forms of abuse—emotional, physical, and sexual abuse as well as neglect—are harmful. Even after the abuse has stopped, the effects remain for a long time. No one asks to be abused, and no one deserves to be abused.

Recognizing abuse

Some victims of abuse do not realize that they are being mistreated. Abuse may be all they have ever known, so the behavior seems "normal" to them. Abusers sometimes tell their victims that they love them or that they are helping them. Abusers may say that the abuse is "just a game." Statements like those can make victims feel confused.

When people know their rights, and understand their physical and emotional needs, they can more easily recognize abuse.

Abuse is frightening, and it may seem impossible to stop. However, it is important for victims to know that help and support are available. No one has to stay in an abusive situation.

Some abusers give their victims money or gifts to make them feel "loved" and to keep them from speaking out about the abuse.

To bring abuse to an end, a victim must first recognize that it is happening and then tell someone about it.

Scared silent

Speaking out about abuse can be difficult. Some victims are afraid to tell anyone. Their abusers may have threatened to hurt them if they don't keep silent. Victims sometimes fear that they will not be believed or helped. They also worry that they will get in trouble. They may not want their abusers to get into trouble, especially if they are family members.

CASE STUDY

Fourteen-year-old Erica was neglected and abused by her parents for several years. Her father abused her sexually. Her mother knew about the sexual abuse but did nothing to stop it. Instead, she often hit Erica and told her that she was bad and worthless. One day, a concerned teacher asked Erica whether she was OK. She broke into tears and told her teacher everything. That was the beginning of the end of the abuse.

Abuse is never the victim's fault. Even so, victims of abuse may feel guilty, embarrassed, or ashamed about being abused. Some victims think that they are responsible for the abuse or that they deserved it. They keep quiet because they fear being blamed.

If a young person is being abused by a family member, others in the family may know what is going on but may not step in to help. Parents, siblings, or other relatives may be too ashamed or frightened to confront the abuser, so they ignore the abuse instead. If abuse is to be stopped, however, it is necessary for someone to speak out, loud and clear.

Victims of abuse should not suffer in silence. Talking to someone may seem scary, but it can be a lifesaver.

Speaking out

Abusers will do anything they can to keep their victims from speaking out about the abuse. Abusers may threaten to hurt the victims or people they care about. An abuser may tell a child that no one will believe his or her claims of abuse. However, speaking out is the most important thing a victim of abuse can do. Reaching out to a trusted relative, teacher, counselor, religious leader, doctor, or friend is the first step on the path to ending abuse and the fear and pain it causes.

It is important to remember that there are people who care and who can help. Victims often disclose their

A trusted friend can be a great source of help and support when someone decides to speak out about abuse or neglect.

experiences of abuse when they are able or when it feels safe. It is never too late to tell, but the sooner a victim speaks out, the sooner the abuse can be stopped. Then the process of healing can begin.

Taking the first step

Some victims live with abuse for a long time. They may think that they do not have the right or the power to ask for help, and they feel discouraged. Eventually, they may reach a point where they cannot cope with the situation any longer. Some people who suffer abuse are unable to eat, sleep, or concentrate. If they are abused by a family member, they may feel too afraid to return home. They may also worry that the abuser will go on to hurt someone else, perhaps a younger sibling. That possibility may finally prompt the victim to tell someone about the abuse.

Sometimes, a friend, a teacher, or a neighbor suspects that a child is being abused. That trusted person may be able to encourage the victim to open up about the experience. People who are sensitive to the abuse of others may have experienced abuse themselves. They can help victims realize that they are not alone.

Where to find help

Several organizations, such as Childhelp, offer support to victims of abuse. Many groups have free telephone helplines operated by

In focus: finding a voice

People who are abused sometimes reveal the abuse unconsciously. It may accidentally "slip out," perhaps in a classroom discussion or during a casual conversation with a friend. At other times, people decide consciously that the time has come to speak out about their experience of abuse.

Victims may feel very alone, but there is always someone who cares and who can help put a stop to abuse and neglect. See page 47 for organizations to contact.

Victims can call a helpline to get the support they need to bring abuse to an end.

trained staff who understand the problems of abuse and who can help. More information about these organizations is available on the Internet or in local phone directories. (See page 47 for a list of child abuse organizations and helplines.)

Sometimes, victims of abuse need to speak to more than one person to get the best possible help. If a victim reveals abuse and no action is taken within a week, he or she should tell someone else—and keep telling until someone provides the help that the victim needs and deserves.

What happens next?

Some people are reluctant to report child abuse; they are afraid to cause trouble for the victim or the victim's family. However, reporting abuse or neglect can protect a child and get help for a family. It may even save a child's life.

Each state has laws requiring certain people to report concerns of child abuse and neglect. Some states identify specific professionals who must report suspected abuse. They typically include social workers, medical and mental health professionals, teachers, and childcare providers. Other states require all people to report their concerns of suspected abuse or neglect. In most states, the person who reports abuse does not have to give his or her name. The child abuser cannot find out who made the report.

When someone reports child abuse, **child protective services** workers offer help. Trained investigators talk to the child and people who know him or her, such as teachers, doctors, and childcare providers. Investigators also speak to the child's family. If the child has been physically or sexually abused, the agency typically calls the police. Only children who are thought to be in immediate danger are removed from a home during the investigation.

The child protection investigators work hard to find out exactly what happened to the victim and whether abuse is likely to happen again. Then agency workers make a plan to provide services that will help the child and keep him or her safe.

Decisions are also made about what will happen to the abuser. Some people who are found to have abused children are offered voluntary help. Other abusers are required by a court to take part

in services that will help keep their children safe. In very serious cases, police may file criminal charges against the abusers.

Victims of abuse should always remember that the abuse is not their fault. What happens to the abuser is not their responsibility, either.

Child protective services can work with families to make sure that young people get the help they need.

Chapter 7: *Recovery from abuse*

Neglect and emotional, physical, and sexual abuse are painful to experience. The effects of abuse are deeply damaging and can last for years. However, victims can and do recover from abuse. Once the victim feels able to speak out, help is available to bring the abuse to an end. No one has to suffer abuse alone.

No one forgets abuse and neglect, but with help, victims can be happy and lead successful lives.

In focus: *safety from abuse*

To stay safe and to help bring abuse to an end, victims should:

- stay as far as they can from an abuser (try not to be alone with the abuser, and do not go anywhere that abuse might happen)
- trust that if something does not feel right, it is not right
- remember that the abuse is not their fault
- tell someone they trust about the abuse, or contact a child abuse helpline
- call the police (dial 911) if they feel they are in immediate danger

A new life

When an instance of abuse becomes known, both the child and the family need help in recovery. The victim and his or her family members may be afraid or feel guilty about what has occurred. Services can include medical care, mental health therapy, and individual, group, or family counseling. Children and families can sometimes benefit from substance abuse programs, marriage counseling, or parenting skills training.

CASE STUDY

Kerri was neglected by her parents and sexually abused by an older cousin. She felt worthless and became depressed. She didn't want to go out or see her old friends, and she was lonely. Kerri was often hungry and tired, and she could not keep up with her schoolwork. She felt desperate.

One day, Kerri learned of an organization to help young people who are abused. She was scared, but she dialed the helpline number. The person who answered her call listened carefully as Kerri spoke. Kerri felt that the helpline counselor believed her and wanted to help. The counselor asked whether Kerri wanted to report the abuse to people who could check into the situation. She explained what might happen as a result. Then she gave Kerri the phone number for the child protective services in her community. The helpline counselor even stayed on the phone and made a three-way call because Kerri was nervous about making a report.

Kerri was surprised at how much other people cared about her. A year later, she feels much better. Her family life has slowly improved, and the sexual abuse has stopped. Kerri feels more confident and has reconnected with some of her old friends. She will never forget the abuse and neglect, but she knows she can move forward.

When a victim's old life of abuse comes to an end, a new and happier life can begin to flourish.

Glossary

acquired immune deficiency syndrome (AIDS): the final stage of infection with human immunodeficiency virus (HIV)

antisocial behavior: actions that differ from socially accepted behavior. Antisocial behavior typically includes fighting, running away from home, abusing drugs or alcohol, and stealing.

child protective services: a government agency that investigates reports of abuse and gives professional support to children and families

coma: a long period of unconsciousness

corporal punishment: physical punishment as a method of discipline. It may include hitting, slapping, and spanking.

corrupting: using one's authority or power to make another person do something wrong or illegal

depression: a mood disorder marked by persistent sadness, inactivity, difficulty in concentration, a significant increase or decrease in appetite and sleep, and feelings of hopelessness

disability: an illness, an injury, or a condition that limits someone's ability to do certain things, such as move about, hear, see, or learn

domestic violence: physical or emotional injury by one family or household member to another

emotional abuse: actions that cause emotional and mental pain and damage to another person

ethnic minorities: groups of people who come from a different background than most people within a country or a society

explicit: very clear, obvious, or detailed

exploitation: victimizing or taking advantage of someone, usually for personal gain

human immunodeficiency virus (HIV): the virus that causes acquired immune deficiency syndrome (AIDS)

hygiene: practices to promote cleanliness and health

indecent exposure: showing one's private body parts in a place where the behavior is offensive

intimidate: to frighten someone, often to cause the person do something

isolation: separation or removal from others

malnutrition: a condition caused by the lack of necessary nourishment from food

nausea: stomach upset with an urge to vomit

neglect: failure to look after the basic needs of a person for whom one is responsible

physical abuse: physical mistreatment of one person by another

pornography: words or pictures that are sexually explicit

prostitute: a person who engages in sexual activity in exchange for money

psychological: relating to the mind and the emotions

seizures: abnormal electrical activity in the brain, which can cause violent shaking and loss of consciousness

self-esteem: confidence and satisfaction in oneself

self-harm: deliberate injury of oneself. It can take many forms, such as cutting, scratching, or burning the skin.

sexual abuse: physical or sexual contact with a person against his or her will

sexually transmitted diseases (STDs): diseases, such as herpes, passed on through sexual contact

shaken baby syndrome: injuries, particularly to the head, caused by violently shaking an infant

stress: mental tension resulting from factors that cause strain or pressure

suffocating: preventing someone from being able to breathe

trauma: an event or an experience that is very upsetting and shocking

vulnerable: liable to be damaged or harmed

Further information

Books to read

Engel, Beverly. *The Emotionally Abusive Relationship.* Hoboken, N.J.: John Wiley & Sons, Inc., 2003.

Lehman, Carolyn. *Strong at the Heart: How It Feels to Heal from Sexual Abuse.* New York: Farrar, Straus and Giroux, 2005.

Mather, Cynthia L. *How Long Does It Hurt? A Guide to Recovering from Incest and Sexual Abuse for Teenagers, Their Friends, and Their Families.* San Francisco: Jossey-Bass, 2004.

Sanders, Pete. *Dealing with Bullying—Choices and Decisions.* London: Franklin Watts, 2007.

Organizations to contact

Childhelp USA
Web site: **www.childhelp.org**
Toll-free helpline: 1-800-4-A-CHILD (1-800-422-4453)
The Childhelp National Child Abuse Hotline operates 24 hours a day, 365 days a year. Hotline counselors are available to help young people, as well as adults, who are worried about children they suspect are being abused or neglected. All calls are free and anonymous.

National Domestic Violence Hotline
Web site: **www.ndvh.org**
Toll-free hotline: 800-799-SAFE (7233)
Hotline advocates are available 24 hours a day for victims and anyone calling on their behalf to provide crisis intervention, safety planning, information, and referrals to agencies in all 50 states.

Helpful web sites

TeensHealth
www.kidshealth.org/teen/your_mind/families/family_abuse.html
TeensHealth (part of the KidsHealth web site) provides teenagers and families with accurate, up-to-date information about abuse and neglect. Content is developed by doctors and other health experts.

National Teen Dating Abuse Helpline
www.loveisrespect.org
This 24-hour national web-based and telephone resource was created to help teens (ages 13 to 18) experiencing dating abuse. The helpline is staffed by both teen and adult advocates. Teens (and parents) can call toll free (866-331-9474) or log on to the interactive web site to receive immediate, confidential assistance and referrals to local resources.

Helpguide
www.helpguide.org/mental/child_abuse_physical_emotional_sexual_neglect.htm
This web site offers information about the four main types of abuse (neglect and physical, emotional, and sexual abuse) and their warning signs, possible causes, and effects. Helpguide also provides tips on preventing and stopping abuse and lists contact information and links to resources for people who need help.

Publisher's note to educators and parents: Our editors have carefully reviewed these web sites to ensure that they are suitable for children. Many web sites change frequently, however, and we cannot guarantee that a site's future contents will continue to meet our high standards of quality and educational value. Be advised that children should be closely supervised whenever they access the Internet.

Index